RULE O LION, RULE THE WORLD AGAIN.

CHARU GUPTA

This book is dedicated to all those who aspire to do good
for humanity by performing the act of leadership.

Contents

Contents

Foreword

Leadership cant not be pursued by hiding. It can only be learnt and practiced by choosing to face the challenges that appear to disturb the governed. The primary duty of a leader is to govern and lead those who are under his/her rule. No amount of shyness will help you to lead but those who act with bravery are always preferred. Let us all apply our bravery to choose humanity. Let us all choose compassion and humanity. Let us all bravely declare that we will pursue humanity. In this book I have covered topics that will help you to decide and form your own opinion about leadership. I have tried to cover all the topics that I could think of to explain the essence of leadership.

ACKNOWLEDGEMENTS

I am thankful to all the leaders from India and abroad for not discouraging a common man to look up to them for encouragement. I hope that the new leaders will learn from them. They are a source of inspiration to all of us.

I

CLIMB THE SUMMIT, THE BIGGEST MOUNTAIN IS YOUR TIMID SELF.

When we aim for leadership positions, the first barrier we have to cross is our timidness. Our timidness is the biggest hurdle on the path of leadership. We have to stop considering ourselves weak and insufficient. A human being is the most powerful agent of change. What you think directs your actions and when your thoughts are constantly fed with courage, your timidness takes a backseat and your strong personality comes to the fore.

Nurture your mind with good thoughts. This will diminish your confusion. Always choose the right because it is the obvious choice to lessen the confusion. It also lessens the burden of not acting and enriches our personality with the power to act.

When you overcome the hurdle of timidness, you are naturally on the path of becoming a leader. Keep moving ahead on the path of your excellence. Excellence leads to experience which further leads to wisdom. The personality so formed is ready to climb any mountain and achieve success.

II

BE A LEADER, THE REAL POWER IS TO DECIDE GOOD FOR OTHERS.

We all feel shy and inhibited when confronted with a challenge. When a challenge suddenly appears, it makes us feel small until we get control of our senses/situation and analyse the problem. After a thorough analysis, we can come to know the real cause. When we overcome the timidness to not act, we get an insight into what should be the solution. Thereafter, the solution becomes accessible. No human in this world is born equipped to handle the challenges. Yes, some are more brave than others. Some kind of training is always required that prepares us to face the challenges. When we train our minds with good thoughts and prepare us physically, we can consider ourselves equipped for the challenge.

Sometimes, life suddenly throws a challenge at us for which we are not prepared. Don't be afraid. Take a deep breath. Calm your mind. Analyse the problem. Do the research. Take the action to get to the solution. We can always expect a good solution when the problem is thoroughly thought out.

A good leader is a solution provider. Nobody is pre-prepared for the problem. The solution is always a result of a leader's knowledge in the given field, wisdom to choose the right and concern for humanity. He will always be presented with different solutions. But when he chooses to make the right decision the result of which is human good, we can say that relevancy is sought. Relevancy is the most important aspect of the decision-making process. It is the sole criterion that determines the correctness of a solution. Relevancy, when sought in terms of humanity is never detrimental to life and does not threaten the human good. Thus, what appears to be a great challenge becomes easy when we seek the solution by guiding the solutions with knowledge, wisdom, sincerity and relevance. These qualities are found to be in abundance in a good leader.

III

THE QUESTION IS NOT WHO WILL LEAD THE CROWD, BUT WHO WILL STAND BY.

Compassion is the best quality of a leader. The crowd may not relate to any unnecessary display of power but the leader who will stand by the public is liked and appreciated by them. There are local issues which when resolved promptly decrease the emotional as well as material burden. These local issues demand immediate attention. The continuance of issues may aggravate the problem. Therefore, addressing these issues promptly helps to alleviate the issue. Moreover, even if the issue is on a large scale the solution sought should answer the problem with a humanitarian concern. The issues largely are similar in different parts of the world. Therefore, a humanitarian point of view will answer the problem for all the population for the same problem.

Thus, a leader with sympathy, empathy and compassion for humans and all other natural resources will surely gain the crowd's attention and will be seen as a true leader. He will be chosen naturally to lead. Because pretence may need some display but true compassion is immediately recognised. A leader who stands by the crowd will be chosen without any confusion, fear of prejudice, and regard for bias. The crowd will experience true freedom and liberty in opting for the leader for their choice of how to live.

IV

PEOPLE ARE NOT JUST A CROWD TO CONTROL, BUT A COLLECTIVE ENTITY THAT CONTROLS YOU.

A leader can not be driven by his whims and fancies. A good leader must be vigilant of local, national and international issues. He should maintain good interaction and connection with the people he wants to lead. He should be aware of their problems. The decisions taken by him should be in consideration for the welfare of humans and the betterment of humanity.

Leadership is a duty to be performed for the betterment of whom you want to lead. It is a responsibility to be undertaken for the benefit of the crowd. The criteria for the decisions to be taken for the welfare of the crowd should be based on the protection of human rights which necessarily means the protection of the human race from illegitimate threats and crimes and a genuine concern for natural resources. Therefore, a leader who is driven by the issues that concern the crowd and issues that affect them directly will be considered a good leader. The solutions sought by him will be beneficial to those being led.

V

WHAT YOU PURSUE DETERMINES YOUR OBEDIENCE, WHO YOU LEAD DETERMINES YOUR DEVOTION

The ideas a leader wants to pursue determine the obedience of the leader. The ideas pursued tell the work being conducted. They tell the direction of the leadership being undertaken. When the interest of the leader is in consonance with the welfare of humanity, we can say that the world is in safe hands and the leadership is answering all the problems pertaining to human upliftment and welfare. When a leader shows his obedience towards human welfare and upliftment, we can be assured that all the right work for human progress will be enforced. The ideas enforced for human welfare will ensure that those being led are happy and contended. The dedication of the leaders towards correct issues will determine the happiness of the public. The public will feel safe under the leadership which ensures a comfortable life for them which essentially means a smooth routine and a life which is less disturbed by any threat. Thus, the obedience of a leader to human progress determines his devotion towards the public he aims to lead.

VI

YOUR PURPOSE IS AS IMPORTANT AS YOUR POWER, FOR THERE IS NO BETTER DECISION THAN TO CHOOSE THE RIGHT.

Power when deprived of the intention to protect and provide is not considered true. The power exerted for the protection of innocent, for the welfare of public, for the development of nations and for the prevalence of peace is the true power. When the purpose associated with the power is appropriate, the effect of the power enforced will be correct. The purpose determines the extent and expanse of the power. The power wielded for the human welfare results in the prevalence of a better and a happy world. The only essential right in the domain of leadership is the decision taken for the protection of human rights and also the protection of other natural resources. In this era the best decisions that we seek are the decisions taken for the protection of human interests and the actions taken for the protection of environment. These right decisions and actions will determine the future of the world. We need a world where abunadnce of natural resources is not compromised and protection of fundamental human rights is ensured. Therefore, when a leader's purpose is to exert power to choose right, he can ensure the longevity of peace, progress, compassion, devotion, love and abundance on the earth.

VII

WHAT MAKES YOU POWERFUL DETERMINES YOUR STRENGTH, THE MORE JUST THE CAUSE IS, THE MORE THE POWER.

The word power is synonymous with leadership. When the exerted leadership is in sync with the causes that affect humans, it renders the strength of belief to the citizens.

Their faith in humanity is restored. A leader is powerful because he can make decisions for the followers. He is the agent that can better their life. They rely on him for their life. Such is the power of someone who intends to take up the position of a leader. Those leaders who gain the trust of public by the virtue of their good decisions and actions are the most loved and appreciated. They are looked up to by the future generations also. The decisions which determine the welfare of humans tells the true power of a leader because the decisions which strengthen the power of humanity are the real indicator of what a leader can accomplish. A leader who works for the sustenance of humanity is the most powerful for he can better the life of his followers not only in his territory but also worldwide by setting up good examples for future leaders also. Those who conduct their actions for conservation of human values have the power to protect humanity and are therefore the ideal examples of leaders for they can lead in the right direction and they are the true examples of power because power is useless when it cannot protect. Simply put, a leader who can protect the cause of humanity is the most powerful.

VIII

WHAT YOU
ACQUIRE
THROUGH YOUR
EXCELLENCE
REFLECTS YOUR
REAL QUALITIES.
IT IS THE ONLY
FACTOR THAT
ENSURES REAL
SUCCESS.

Excellence is a virtue that can only be earned by the sheer hard work of the seeker. There is no other way. It is the best distinction a man can earn because it is the only qualification earned by his actions. Just as the precious metals and gems have to be extracted, polished and designed for their value so is transformation required by a man to acquire excellence. Time is no constraint when the aim is excellence. Work is the only master. Perseverance is the key. Tenacity to the cause to be pursued can ensure your excellence.

Anything that is acquired by the quality of your hard work which is in consonance with the principles of humanity, purity of intentions and appropriateness of the subject for which the excellence is sought can never fail to succeed the pursuer. The essence of excellence, acquired in consideration of the mentioned criteria determines the qualities of the seeker. It surely sets a good example for others when excellence is dedicated to provide solutions to humanity. It increases the extent and expanse of your success when it benefits the entire world.

IX

A GOOD LEADER IS A CHERISHED POSSESSION, FOR HE IS NOT A LIABILITY BUT AN ASSET.

A leader who works for the welfare of humans is an asset. His ideas and his work leave a good impression on the followers. He becomes famous amongst his followers as well as citizens from other areas. The human heart understands the language of kindness. When a leader dedicates his ideology to the welfare of humans, the impression created by his personality impresses his followers to practice the same. This kindness spreads to the entire world as an example and people start following him. As they say, happiness is contagious. It relieves the burden of agony from a human mind and restores his faith in humanity. By being a follower of a good leader we can be assured that goodness will protect us all. Goodness lessens the burden of distrust from society. The more we trust our fellow citizens, the better life we can ensure. A leader who ensures the prevalence of good in a society is doing a great job. He is ensuring the trust of people in humanity and he is an example who can be trusted to be followed for the creation of a healthy society where qualities like kindness and affection can sustain their presence. Therefore, he is an asset.

X

GOOD LEADERS
DETERMINE THE
CHOICES OF THE
PEOPLE, FOR THE
CITIZENS ARE
THE MOST
OBEDIENT TO THE
ONE WHO LEAD.

When we present ourselves as an option to be chosen by the people to lead them, we are giving them a chance to decide. They decide whether the ideas and promises presented by us will suit them or not. They can make a choice for their betterment and how they can achieve that. This choice determines the type of leadership they want and it is solely their power and right to choose. We can tell them about our ideas but it is up to them to choose us or not. As a leader, it is our duty to inform them about the good we can give them and also the benefits of that good in the long run. When we present our ideas to them, we must ensure that the relevancy of our ideas should not compromise the ideas of humanity. We must make them aware and not merely entice them to believe us. Promises should consider human good as the top priority. The self-interest will serve no purpose for a leader who considers all life equal. Therefore, this interaction between leader and followers should enlighten both - the leader to have a more devoted outlook towards humanity and the followers to be made confident that their welfare is the utmost priority of the chosen. Thus, better ideas ensure better obedience which should be understood in terms of the devotion of the leaders and followers to achieve a happy, healthy, compassionate, devoted and affectionate society.

XI

LET US CREATE MORE LEADERS, WE NEED GOOD DECISION-MAKERS.

We should not consider a select class for the leadership roles. People who are empathetic about social issues and human welfare should be given a chance. Governance is not just a system designed to carry out only diplomacy. It is a system meant for the upliftment and welfare of citizens by the administration of work enshrined in the constitution of the country and also for the discharge of duties as directed to persons concerned for the achievement of the same. Consideration for the betterment of humanity and the welfare of citizens and other natural resources and appropriate and judicious use of all other means to achieve the development of the nation and progress of the country while having a big heart for the entire world are the main ideas of governance. Leaders are essentially decision-makers. Those who can decide better for the pursuance of the idea of governance and administration must come forward to choose the profession. We need good decision-makers who can be trusted for the protection of life on the earth. This system of administration must protect the living for the continuance of all other functions that are considered to be necessary. There is no development without life and there is no progress without humanity. Protection of the innocent from illegitimate threats and preservation of innocence in the human psyche is the most important part of this duty of governance and must be carried out with full empathy and dedication to prevent the loss of humanity from the world.

XII

EDUCATION IS
THE MOST
REQUIRED
QUALITY IN A
LEADER BECAUSE
YOU MAY BELONG
TO ANY FIELD,
BUT THE
EXCELLENCE
ACQUIRED

DETERMINES HOW WELL YOU WILL LEAD

Excellence is a prerequisite for a man to be a leader. He may belong to any field. The leadership sought can only be provided when he is excellent in his chosen field of study and profession. Followers will consider him a role model only when he can provide the necessary inspiration to them. That can only be achieved when the leader has earned his excellence by creating the best benchmark in his field or profession. Education is the first step to excellence. No student can learn, understand, comprehend and create without learning the basics of his subject. Leadership when sought with the quality of excellence will never deceive or cheat the followers because they will be learning from the experience of their leader. They will have the examples of the achievements of their leader that they could apply to their own journey and create even better examples on their own and the best version of themselves. Thus, a leader creates more leaders when the followers are not confused about the identity of their leaders that is prefixed with excellent.

XIII

DON'T BE SHY TO LEAD, YOU ARE THE ONLY SOLUTION TO THE PROBLEM YOU PERCEIVE.

Perception is the quality of an inquisitive mind. He who analyses the problem with intelligence has a good perception. In the realm of human authority, perception of problems and seeking the correct solution is a good practice. Perception is a very important tool for leadership. A correct comprehension of problems makes us reach the solution with correct relevancy. Therefore, those who perceive the problem correctly should not be shy to lead and give and implement their suggestions. We need leaders whose perception matches the sought solution for to achieve relevancy we can not begin with wrong notions and irrelevant intelligence. Therefore, a leader who seeks relevancy in the principles of humanity and the welfare of humans can never go wrong with his perception that a life nurtured and nourished can inspire many others with the same healthy emotion whereas a life tortured disheartens not only the sufferer but the entire generation.

XIV

TIMIDNESS IS THE ENEMY OF LEADERSHIP, A LION IS NEVER SHY TO ATTACK.

The greed of power is the weakness of the deprived and deficient. Those who are deprived always get lured by the idea of power. Power lures especially those who fantasize it as the only source of compensation for their personal deficiences and weaknesses. In reality, power is the most contrary to fantasy. The power I mentioned earlier in the paragraph means leadership. The act of being a leader is the most realistic job in the world. There is nothing to fantasize about it. The leaders who aim to be powerful must be protective of their ideology. Because there will be many who would fantasize of themselves being in that leader's position. But the status of being a leader can only be earned by working hard for the issues related to those being governed. Therefore, it is okay to defend your ideology but it is ideal to dare the adversary. Keep yourself ready. As ready as a lion to protect yourself from the greedy. No timidness should be shown to the adversary while protecting your ideology and those who believe in you. And always be guided by the principles of humanity for the ideal ideology is to work for the welfare of humans and other natural resources.

XV

PEOPLE ARE ALWAYS JEALOUS OF THE STRONG, BECAUSE OF THEIR OWN DEFICIENCIES.

Power lures. Ambitious people either earn it or snatch it. Ambition, when nurtured with the right intentions and emotions, makes you work hard and make you excel in your chosen field of profession. Those who have weak personalities always think of shortcuts to realize their dreams and fulfil their aspirations of being powerful. The word power is to be understood in terms of performance. Those who perform can deliver the results. Whereas, those who snatch are a cause of disturbance for the governed because those who follow can not seek the right results from them. This field of governance is more about delivering the right to the living. To deliver the amenities, justice and opportunities is the real work of a leader. Whereas, those who snatch are deprived of the courage to perform and are deficient in bravery to deliver justice and always fall short of providing the necessary opportunities and amenities to those who are governed. Therefore, it is necessary for a future leader to go through the process of transformation and that essentially means to know that his/her duty is to primarily work for the welfare of humanity and to ensure availability of resources for future generations.

XVI

HUMANS HAVE THE POWER TO DETERMINE THE FUTURE BECAUSE WE HAVE THE OPTION TO CHOOSE AND THE WILL TO DECIDE.

HUMANS HAVE THE POWER TO DETERMINE THE FUTURE

BECAUSE WE HAVE THE OPTION TO CHOOSE AND THE WILL TO DECIDE

THOSE WHO EXERCISE BOTH WITH A CONCERN FOR HUMANITY

CAN MAKE THE WORLD A BETTER AND A HAPPY PLACE.

The future is the choice we opt to make decisions for the governed. We humans are the most powerful agents of change. We should deliberately choose the option/solution that works for the welfare and upliftment of humans. A leader always has the power to decide. Those who exercise their will to choose the best for humanity are always considered the best decision-makers. A common man always relies on the leader for the decisions to be taken for his betterment. His reliance should not be compromised. When we exert the power to protect the innocent we are working with divine guidance to protect and save. That is how a real leader validates his power. Let us all pledge to make this world a better and happy place. Let us all be guided by the principles of nature and humanity that only compassion for life and sympathy for living can save mankind. Let us begin the change now. Let us all be the heroes. Let love prevail.

XVII

Rule O Lion, Rule The World Again.

Rule O Lion, Rule the World Again

 Rule O Lion,

 Rule the world again

 Your presence is awaited to free our souls again

 Arise from the shadows of your past

 Tear off the spider's web that has kept you hidden from your kingdom vast

 The glory of your valour beseeches your will to act.

 The throne of the king awaits your presence to protect.

 You shall be the ruler of the world

 Your glorious acts will be sung by the whole earth

 Justice will be done

 Innocence will be protected

 In your kingdom, the truth shall prevail and honesty will be rewarded

 Rule O Lion

 Rule the world again

Your presence is awaited to free our souls again
To release the fear from the minds of your subjects
To let the birds sing the sweet song of connect
Where the souls are not tethered to the ideology of abomination
And we are free to live and work without any subjugation.
Rule O Lion,
Rule the world again
Your presence is awaited to free our souls again
Let your roar awake the world to a new dawn
Where the guidance of enlightenment takes us to the pedestal of a new song
Which is sung by all alike
To lead us on the path of correct and upright
Where humanity guides the voice of every heart
And there is no confusion to the relevance of a new start
Where all are a part of the chorus of god's will
That nothing except humanity will beguile
None shall suffer from the hands of tyranny or crime
All are busy creating a beautiful life with perfect rhyme
Rule O Lion,
Rule the world again
Your presence is awaited to free our souls again